The

31 Day Prayer Project

for Spiritual Growth

Stephanie A. Mayberry

All scriptures used in this text are taken from
the King James Version Bible

COPYRIGHT © 2023 STEPHANIE A. MAYBERRY
ALL RIGHTS RESERVED. NO PART OF THIS BOOK MAY BE REPRODUCED OR TRANSMITTED IN ANY FORM OR BY ANY MEANS, ELECTRONIC, MECHANICAL, INCLUDING PHOTOCOPYING, RECORDING, OR BY INFORMATION STORAGE AND RETRIEVAL SYSTEM – EXCEPT BY A REVIEWER WHO MAY QUOTE BRIEF PASSAGES IN A REVIEW TO BE PRINTED IN A MAGAZINE OR NEWSPAPER OR ON A WEBSITE – WITHOUT WRITTEN PERMISSION FROM THE AUTHOR.

ISBN: 9798874410797

Printed in the USA

.

Books by Stephanie A. Mayberry

My Testimony

101 Simple Ways to Minister to Others

7 Steps to a Godly Marriage

Praying God's Word: For Teens and Young Adults

31 Days of Praise for Depression

31 Day Prayer Project for Spiritual Growth

HEALING FOR THE BATTERED SPIRIT SERIES

My Story is not Unique (a story about domestic violence)

Why I Stayed: Ministering to the Battered Spirit

More Valuable than Sparrows: Healing for the Battered Spirit

THE CHRISTIAN ASPIE SERIES

Fringe: My Life as a Spirit-Filled Christian with Asperger's Syndrome

More Fringe: My Growth as a Spirit-Filled Christian with Asperger's Syndrome

The Christian Aspie: Notes from the Blog

DEDICATION

I dedicate this book to all who want a closer, more personal, more intimate relationship with Yeshua. He is life, He is light, He is love and the closer you walk with Him, the more like Him you will be. The road will not always be easy, but the rewards are so great!

Praise Yeshua!

Dear Reader,

If the words in my books speak to you, resonate with you, touch you, please know it isn't really me, it is God speaking to you.

See, I am just a vessel that He uses to convey His message to you, to others. I am no great writer; I am just the obedient hand that holds the pen for the greatest author of all – my God.

He alone deserves all of the praise, all the glory.

Thank you so much for your support and encouragement. Each and every email, every word, every letter is such a treasure to me! I pray for your continued growth in your relationship with God. Forever walk in His Word and you will know blessings beyond your imagination.

God is so good, isn't He?

Stephanie Mayberry

TABLE OF CONTENTS

Day 1	Closer relationship with Yeshua	1
Day 2	Deeper understanding of who I am in Yeshua	7
Day 3	Increased hunger for the word of God	13
Day 4	Help me to seek the things of God first	19
Day 5	Better understanding of scripture	25
Day 6	Fully understand what happened at the cross	31
Day 7	Healing	37
Day 8	Overcome fear	43
Day 9	Develop a richer, more fulfilling prayer life	49
Day 10	Build my faith	55
Day 11	Forgiveness	61

Day 12	Give me a new heart	67
Day 13	Take better care of my temple	73
Day 14	Lead me to a body of believers	79
Day 15	Allow God to fulfill His purpose in my life	85
Day 16	Repent	91
Day 17	Become a better disciple	97
Day 18	God's will not mine	103
Day 19	Deeper understanding of my authority in Yeshua	109
Day 20	Understand my spiritual gifts	115
Day 21	Put the love of God in my heart	121
Day 22	Purify me so that I may embody and display all the fruits of the spirit	127

Day 23	Deeper understanding that everything is spiritual	133
Day 24	Realizing my power to defeat the enemy	139
Day 25	Be more fully submitted to the Holy Spirit	145
Day 26	I am separate from the world	151
Day 27	Help me weather the storms better	157
Day 28	Working out my own salvation	163
Day 29	Be holy as He is holy	169
Day 30	Help me to abide in Yeshua	175
Day 31	Help me bear good fruit	181

DAY 1

> Behold, I stand at the door, and knock: if any man hear my voice, and open the door, I will come in to him, and will sup with him, and he with me.
>
> REVELATION 3:20

DAY 1
Closer relationship with Yeshua
Revelation 3:20

Lord, I want a closer, deeper, more meaningful relationship with You. I give my life to You. Every word, every action, every thought is for You and to glorify You.

I need You, Lord. I need You to mold me and shape me into who You want me to be. I hear You knocking, I hear Your voice. Please come to me and be with me.

Help me draw closer to You. I want that deep relationship with You.

Help me as I study Your word, Lord. Write Your words on my heart and infuse Your spirit with mine so that You are my thoughts, my actions, my words so that I live and breathe with You.

Make me like You so that when people look at me it's Your face that they see. I want my life to reflect You in such a way that people want to know You.

I want to be that light so that they ask where my peace comes from, my joy, my contentment.

That can only come from having a relationship with You, a true relationship that puts me on my knees in prayer and draws me into Your word each day. I want to know You; I want more of You. I need You, Lord.

I ask You, please let this month of prayer, this month of seeking You, be fruitful and profitable. Guide me as I seek You and open my understanding so that I can have the closeness and intimacy with You that I so desperately need and desire.

Amen.

DAY 2

> Therefore if any man be in Christ, he is a new creature: old things are passed away; behold, all things are become new.
>
> 2 CORINTHIANS 5:17

DAY 2
Deeper understanding of who I am in Yeshua
2 Corinthians 5:17

Lord, I want You to define me. I want my identity to be in You, not the world.

But I want to know who that person is, that new creature in You. I want to understand this transformed life that You have given me because in knowing who I am in You I will draw closer to You.

I want to understand who I am in You, what purpose You have for my life, and what You want me to become.

I want to fulfill that purpose You have for my life. Use me, Lord, I submit fully to You.

I know I can't live without You.

I know I am not whole without You.

Lord, I put You above everything. There is nothing greater, nothing higher, nothing more important than You.

Mold me and shape me. Move in me and on me and through me so that Your ways become my ways and Your thoughts become my thoughts.

Help me to understand what I am becoming in You. I know it is ongoing and the more I reach for You, the more You will draw me to You.

Put people in my path who love me enough to help me grow in You, people who know Your truth and are fully submitted to You. Give them a burden to pray for me, for who I am and who I am becoming in You.

I want You to draw me in to You now, Yeshua.

I want all that You have for me and I only want to serve You.

Amen

DAY 3

> As newborn babes, desire the sincere milk of the word, that ye may grow thereby:
> If so be ye have tasted that the Lord is gracious.
>
> 1 PETER 2:2-3

DAY 3
Increased hunger for the word of God
1 Peter 2:2-3

Lord, I hunger for Your word, because I want more of You.

Give me an increased hunger for Your word.

Give me a hunger for Your truth.

I want to know You, know who You are.

I want to be the person You created me to be and I want the promises that You have poured into Your holy scriptures. I know that I can only have them by obedience to You which begins with praying without ceasing and studying to show myself approved.

Only then will I be able to fulfill the purpose that You have for me, for my life.

Only then will I truly know You and have the relationship with You that You desire.

Your word is living and active, sharper than a two-edged sword.

It is a lamp unto my feet and a light unto my path.

It is forever and will forever sustain me, guide me, and mold me so that I am more like You.

Open my heart, my understanding of Your word. Bring Your holy scriptures to life and write them on my heart so that they are a part of me, so that when I speak it is Your word that comes forth.

I desire the milk of Your word so that I can grow - grow in You.

I have tasted and seen that the Lord is good.

And I want more.

Never stop pouring Your word into me.

I want more.

DAY 4

> But seek ye first the kingdom of God, and his righteousness; and all these things shall be added unto you.
>
> MATTHEW 6:33

DAY 4
Help me to seek the things of God first
Matthew 6:33

I love You, Lord.

I want You to be first in my life.

I want to seek You first in all that I do. I want the things of God above all else.

But sometimes the enemy puts things in my path to try to distract me and make me turn my eyes off of You and I lose my focus.

And sometimes I get in my own way. My spirit is willing, but my flesh is weak. I get distracted by things my flesh wants – even when I know it's just a distraction.

Sometimes my flesh wins.

Help me to overcome the enemy's games so that I can keep my eyes heavenward, keep my focus on You.

Help me overcome my flesh so that I choose YOU and YOUR WILL instead of my own. Strengthen me, give me wisdom, and help me to grow in You.

Help me to understand and remember that ANYTHING I put before You is idolatry.

You MUST be first and foremost in my life because only then can I truly love.

Because if I don't have You, I don't have love.

But more than that, I know I can't live without You. I know You will guide me, protect me, shelter me, cover me, and raise me up so that I can fulfill all of the plans that You have for me.

I want to always, always seek You first.

DAY 5

> But grow in grace, and in the knowledge of our Lord and Saviour Jesus Christ. To him be glory both now and for ever. Amen.
>
> 2 PETER 3:18

DAY 5
Better understanding of scripture
2 Peter 3:18

Lord, I want to grow in grace.

I want to grow in YOU.

I want to grow in the knowledge of my Lord, Yeshua.

So, I want a deeper, better understanding of scripture, of Your word. I want to delve into Your word and study it, to know the truth of the holy scripture You have given me.

Give me a supernatural understanding through Your Holy Spirit.

Open my eyes so that Your word is made clear.

I want to understand.

I ask You to write Your words on my heart but also let them live in my spirit so that they are a part of me. I want them to color and shape everything I think and say and do.

Let me see with perfect clarity how Your word applies to my life, to all the circumstances and situations I encounter.

Mold me and shape me so that when people see me they see You. Let Your thoughts become my thoughts so that I may have a mind of Yeshua Messiah always and in all seasons.

Just give me understanding as I study and let every word become a part of me.

For this is how I will know You.

This is how I will be intimate with You.

This is how You will direct my life.

So, open my understanding of Your word today.

I just want more and more of You.

DAY 6

> But God commendeth his love toward us, in that, while we were yet sinners, Christ died for us.
>
> ROMANS 5:8

DAY 6
Fully understand what happened at the cross
Romans 5:8

Lord, I want to fully understand what happened at the cross. I know You died for our sins, for MY sins, but I want to fully comprehend it.

I know that there was so much more that happened there.

You became the sacrificial lamb so that my sins could be forgiven through faith, obedience, and grace in You instead of the works of sacrifice done in the Temple.

I know this in my head, but I want to *know* it in my heart!

I desperately need a revelation of the love of Yehovah God. I need to understand just how much You love me – and I know it was carried out at the cross. I just need to see it, to KNOW it.

Open my eyes and increase my faith so that I may know this, of Your unending, unconditional love, and rest in Your truth.

I know that You died for all of us while we were yet sinners. You died for everyone from the holiest saint to the most heinous criminal – and it is Your will that they, that we, ALL be saved!

You prayed for those who crucified You – asking mercy for them even as they mocked and tortured You.

I want to be like You, have that love and grace inside me so that I can be selfless and see the soul instead of the person. I want those new eyes!

I want to have the grace that can only come from You, the grace that allows me to pray for my enemies and bless them.

I thank You, Lord, for giving Your life, for Your sacrifice, for loving me even when I have not been at my best, even when I forgot about You or outright rejected You. Thank You for not giving up on me and always calling me back home.

Let me reflect this loving nature to everyone I encounter so that they are impacted and want to know this joy I have – the joy I have in You.

DAY 7

> For I will restore health unto thee, and I will heal thee of thy wounds, saith the Lord; because they called thee an Outcast, saying, This is Zion, whom no man seeketh after.
>
> JEREMIAH 30:17

DAY 7
Healing
Jeremiah 30:17

Lord, You are the great healer and I need You now. Heal me physically, mentally, and spiritually. I give myself over fully to You, move on me now, please, Lord. Move in me and through me, healing every part, even the wounds I am not aware of.

I know that Your great healing power is mighty and You want me whole, so I ask You today, touch me, Lord. Heal me.

For healing will prepare me to serve You better, to stand more staunchly for You.

Healing will allow the forgiveness to flow from me so that I may be forgiven by You.

Healing will open me up to minister to others who have walked a path similar to mine.

When the body heals the scar tissue that forms is tougher, fortifying that part of the body, making it stronger than it was before. It is the same regardless of where the healing takes place, the body, the heart and emotions, psychology, or spirit. It is all the same, stronger, tougher.

I need that!

I need You!

I need that healing touch so that I am stronger, better, tougher than I was before. For that is what will form my ministry and I need to be completely healed – and fortified – in those areas so that I can help others who are hurt too.

Let Your Holy Spirit wash over me and heal all the places where I am bruised and broken and cut. Heal those wounds that can be seen and those I've hidden in secret places to carry the pain that keeps me from having the relationship that You desire with me.

I thank You for Your healing and all You do in my life.

DAY 8

> Fear thou not; for I am with thee: be not dismayed; for I am thy God: I will strengthen thee; yea, I will help thee; yea, I will uphold thee with the right hand of my righteousness.
>
> ISAIAH 41:10

DAY 8
Overcome fear
Isaiah 41:10

Lord, You tell us over and over to fear not. Throughout Your word, You remind me that You are with me.

Your word says that fear is a spirit You did not give me.

I want to be free from the spirit!

I want to be free from that bondage!

I don't want to be fear's prisoner anymore!

Yehovah, move on me in a mighty way! Move in me and through me, purging any fear that is polluting my spirit. Take with it the anxiety, the worry, the tension, the stress because I don't want to be afraid anymore!

I need You, Lord! I know that fear has been here a long time. I accepted it and even welcomed it at times, but in order to live more fully in You, I must let it go.

I must remove fear from my spirit, my mind, my vocabulary, my actions and replace it with Your love.

I must stop speaking fear into my life and start speaking LIFE – the life You promise.

I want the life that You want for me but in order for that to happen fear has to go.

Draw closer to me, Yehovah. I want a right relationship with You.

Because when I have Your love in me, there is no room for fear. Your word promises that and that is what I want today!

Thank You for molding and shaping me, for helping me get rid of those things within me that are not pleasing to You, that are not of You.

Starting with fear.

Take it, Lord! Take my fear and replace it with faith!

DAY 9

> Pray without ceasing.
>
> 1 THESSALONIANS 5:17

DAY 9
Develop a richer, more fulfilling prayer life
1 Thessalonians 5:17

Teach me to pray, Lord. Help me to develop a richer, more fulfilling prayer life.

I realize that it begins by meeting You daily, praying daily, praying without ceasing.

And I understand that praying without ceasing is about the relationship, a constant communion with You, my spirit joined to Your spirit – and that is praying without ceasing – because my spirit will always be communing with You.

That is the prayer I want.

Help me to quiet the busy chatter, my hectic life, and learn how to stop, be still, and touch You.

I desire more of You, Lord, to be closer to You. I need that time alone with You so I can know You, and have a deeper relationship with You.

And I will open my mouth and speak aloud, for the power of life and death is in the tongue. I will begin to praise You. I will forgive all who have wronged me so that You will forgive me and hear my prayers.

I pray for Your will in my life, that Your will always be done. For to be outside of Your will is to be separated from You – and I don't want that.

I pray for Your provision in my life and thank You for Your faithfulness and love.

I lift others up to You for their various needs and always, ALWAYS, the salvation of their souls.

I just want to be close to You, Lord. I want to know You.

And it starts by opening my mouth and beginning to pray.

DAY 10

> Now faith is the substance of things hoped for, the evidence of things not seen.
>
> HEBREWS 11:1

DAY 10
Build my faith
Hebrews 11:1

Lord, I need You to build my faith. Your word says that I am to trust in You for ALL THINGS.

But sometimes that is so hard even though You promise over and over that You will provide for my needs.

But sometimes You seem so far away.

Increase my faith so that regardless of the circumstances before me I can hold on to Your steadfastness, Your promises that You will NEVER leave me or forsake me.

Give me the faith of Abel to give You a more excellent sacrifice.

Give me the faith of Enoch so I may be translated for my faithfulness.

Give me the faith of Noah that I may hear Your voice and obey even those things not yet seen.

Give me the faith of Abraham that I will go where You send me even though I don't know why I am going.

Give me the faith of Sara that I believe in Your promises even when it looks impossible.

Give me the faith of Abraham to willingly sacrifice those things You ask even though they are dear to me.

Give me the faith of Isaac to bless concerning things to come.

Give me the faith of Isaac to bless that You would fulfill Your promises Your own way and in Your own time.

Give me the faith of Jacob that I may bless and not give in to fear.

Give me the faith of Joseph that I believe You will bring good out of the most dire of circumstances.

Give me the faith of Moses to walk in obedience to You even though the obstacles seem insurmountable – to keep Your Sabbaths and keep Your feasts forever.

Give me the faith of Rahab to obey God rather than man.

I want to have unshakable, immovable faith in You. Help me to find that faith, to grow it, to learn to live in it in all that I do.

DAY 11

> But I say unto you, Love your enemies, bless them that curse you, do good to them that hate you, and pray for them which despitefully use you, and persecute you
>
> MATTHEW 5:44

DAY 11
Forgiveness
Matthew 5:44

Lord, I know You have said to love my enemies. I know that You said if I don't forgive those who wrong me then You won't forgive me.

But it is so hard!

Lord, help me to forgive. Help me to do as You say I should and love my enemies, bless them, and do good to them even though they hate me and curse me. Help me to pray for them as You say I should, even though they persecute me and despitefully use me.

In my flesh, in my carnality, *in my humanness*, I don't want to love them, Lord. And I certainly don't want to pray for them! But I know I have to because You commanded it.

I know I have to because I want You to forgive me.

And I know I have to forgive them because, at the end of the day, they too are souls that You want to see saved.

You died for them just as You died for me.

So, I need You to please put Your love for them into my heart so that I can love them as You do and see them through Your eyes.

Because You are love and if I have Your spirit in me then I am love too.

So, help me to forgive others just as You have forgiven me, with grace and mercy and lovingkindness.

DAY 12

> A new heart also will I give you, and a new spirit will I put within you: and I will take away the stony heart out of your flesh, and I will give you an heart of flesh.
>
> EZEKIEL 36:26

DAY 12
Give me a new heart
Ezekiel 36.26

Lord, I need a new heart. I need my stony heart taken away and I need You to replace it with a heart of flesh.

I want to have in my new heart the love that You feel for others.

You are love so when Your spirit is within me then I am love too.

But I need Your spirit in me every minute of every day. I need it to draw me closer to You and to continue changing me – changing my heart.

Plow my heart right now, Lord! Make it tender so that You can sow the seeds of Your word within me and write them upon this heart. I want to receive it, to receive You.

Search my heart and root out the things that are not pleasing to You and cut them off. Reveal them to me so that I will not fall into that sin again so that I can become more like You.

Help me to keep not just my heart, but also my mind turned toward You and Your ways.

I want to be Yours, one of Your people and I want You to be my God.

Give me a new heart that is removed from this world and walks with You. I want to speak Your words, think Your thoughts, and do Your work with my hands.

Oh, Lord, I want a heart of flesh that is tender to others and wise in Your ways!

I want to be like You.

And it starts with this new heart.

DAY 13

> What? know ye not that your body is the temple of the Holy Ghost which is in you, which ye have of God, and ye are not your own?
> For ye are bought with a price: therefore glorify God in your body, and in your spirit, which are God's.
>
> 1 CORINTHIANS 6:19-20

DAY 13
Take better care of my temple
1 Corinthians 6:19-20

Lord, my body is Your temple, the temple of the Holy Spirit – Your spirit.

My body belongs to You.

I have a responsibility to take good care of it.

I commit to taking better care of Your temple, Lord. Please help me become a better steward of this body You have given me so that I may be a better witness, be healthy, and have more energy to go out and teach Your word.

Lord, temptation is everywhere with unhealthy foods and practices, and I ask You right now to help me eat healthier, get better, more restful sleep, to protect my health and wellness both mentally and physically.

I don't want to defile this temple in any way, be it what I eat, drink, see, listen to, or allow my mind to entertain. Please help me to avoid those things that are not pleasing to You, those things of the world, because I know that it is all just spiritual pollution, and it will affect my walk with You.

Help me avoid and better manage any stress in my life. Stress is hard on the body, but it is also a tool of the enemy to distract me from serving You as I should. It can affect my ministry, my life, my relationships, and my physical body. I realize that the devil will try to steal my shalom, my peace.

Renew my joy in You, my passion, my imagination, my excitement.

I hereby declare that he will not touch me or my family!

Draw me closer to You so that I may keep Your temple well-maintained and healthy.

DAY 14

> Not forsaking the assembling of ourselves together, as the manner of some is; but exhorting one another: and so much the more, as ye see the day approaching.
>
> HEBREWS 10:25

DAY 14
Lead me to a body of believers
Hebrew 10:25

Lord, lead me to a body of believers who have a hunger for Your truth, who want to know more of You, and who live for You with every breath in their body.

Guide me to a body that worships You in spirit and in truth, who rightly divides the word, and seeks for You to write Your words on their hearts.

Whether it's a gathering in a home like the Acts church or a gathering in another structure, remove from my mind any preconceived notions of how "church" should work and just lead me to truth – Your truth.

Let me know them by the fruit they bear and bring me to a body that will edify me and raise me up to become the disciple You want me to be.

Lead me to a body where I can identify my spiritual gifts and learn how to use them for Your glory, for Your furtherance of the kingdom, for leading others to You.

Lead me to a body where they heal the sick, deliver those in bondage, and war in the spirit against the hell that wants to rob us of our joy, our peace, and our families.

Make us strong, Lord. Bind us together and lead us into the coming days that are filled with uncertainty in the world.

Remind us that the only thing, the ONLY THING we can believe in, depend on, and trust is YOU.

DAY 15

> For I know the thoughts that I think toward you, saith the Lord, thoughts of peace, and not of evil, to give you an expected end.
>
> JEREMIAH 29:11

DAY 15
Allow God to fulfill His purpose in my life
Jeremiah 29:11

Lord, I cry out to You now. You knew me before You formed me. You know the plans You have for me.

Help me to come in line with Your plans for my life.

Help me to discover the purpose You have for me, for my life.

Help me to understand that purpose and give me courage, strength, wisdom, and boldness as I pursue it.

You have numbered my days, Lord and You have promised to fulfill every purpose that You have for me as long as I am faithful to You.

Help me to choose You, always You.

I know that it is my choice and my choice only. I know it is my decision, my will, my way. But the world is full of distractions and things to grab my attention – things that may take me off of the path You have set for me.

Please help me stay grounded and on that path!

Give me a heart for You, a mind for You. Put a desire deep within me to always, always seek Your face first.

Help protect me from temptation and when it is put before me, please give me a way of escape. I don't want to pursue it; I want to escape to You.

You, Lord, are my haven, my resting place, my refuge, my rock.

I want to please You. I want to be all that You want me to be.

Mold me and shape me so that I will be. I give myself to You.

DAY 16

> Repent ye therefore, and be converted, that your sins may be blotted out, when the times of refreshing shall come from the presence of the Lord.
>
> ACTS 3:19

DAY 16
Repent
Acts 3:19

Lord, I know that Your word says in order to be forgiven by You I must repent of my sins before You.

Humble me so that I am ready to repent whenever I sin. It is not my intention to sin, but this human flesh is not yet perfected. Help me, Lord, to walk the path You have laid out for me, to walk in Your footsteps, to do what is good and right and holy in Your eyes.

Humble me so that I am not too proud or haughty for that restricts my repentance. Give me a repentant heart that is as quick to forgive as it is to seek forgiveness.

Let all my ways reflect a heart and mind for You.

Mold me, shape me, and guide me. Help me to understand the depth and gravity of repentance that goes far beyond simply saying "I'm sorry."

Help me to turn around, turn away from sin – to go forth and sin no more.

Repentance is not just seeking forgiveness; it is *seeking change*. It is enacting change in my heart and in my mind so that I don't repeat the sins of my past.

Help me to find the reverence in the act and make it quick to spring to my lips when needed.

I open my mouth to declare that I seek to be holy for You are holy and I long to obey Your commands.

Repentance is holiness. True repentance is holiness.

I long to be holy as You are holy.

DAY 17

> And he saith unto them, Follow me, and I will make you fishers of men
>
> MATTHEW 4:19

DAY 17
Become a better disciple
Matthew 4:19

Lord, I want to be a better disciple to You. I want to follow You. I want to be a fisher of men.

I know that it is Your will for all believers to be disciples, that living for You is an active, living existence.

I know that You don't just expect but command that everyone who chooses You, to live for You, should actively go out and reach the lost, minister to the lost, and lead people to You.

Make me a better disciple.

Teach me to pray, Lord, for the people I know and the ones I don't. Make me bold so that I will approach people and offer to pray for them.

Make me bold, Lord, so I am quick and confident to share Your good news with everyone.

Give me wisdom so that when I encounter those who reject You I will not waste time convincing a settled mind and can shake the dust off my feet and seek out the hungry.

Bring the hungry to me, Lord! Put those in my path who are hungry for You, who want to know You.

Send to me the ones who are truly hungry for You, not only for what You can do for them or what I can do for them but those who want a true and deep relationship with You.

Even if they are searching for something but don't know what – send them to me so I can share You with them, show them Your face.

Mold me and shape me into the disciple that You want me to be.

DAY 18

> And he said, Abba, Father, all things are possible unto thee; take away this cup from me: nevertheless not what I will, but what thou wilt.
>
> MARK 14:36

DAY 18
God's will not mine
Mark 14:36

Lord, You knew me before You formed me. You know my ways, my thoughts, my beginning, and my end. You know the outcome of every choice I make long before I make it.

And You know what is best for me.

I never want to be out of Your will, Lord. I never want to walk in that dry place and feel so far from You.

Help me stay in Your will and help me to keep my gaze focused on You. I don't want to be distracted by the world because that just causes discontent and frustration.

I don't want to follow my heart, to pursue my own will because that just leads to carnality, death, and a life separated from You.

I don't want the desolation and despair of living outside of Your will. I know You have a plan for me, You have a life already laid out for me. All I need to do is step into it, to live it.

And all of it is to glorify You.

What more could I ask?

I want to keep my eyes on You, walking in Your will.

I want to please You, to be approved by You, to be everything that You want. But I need clear direction. I need You to speak Your will into my life right now and always.

Open all doors that lead to Your will, Lord, and close all doors that lead away from it.

Help me so that I do not stray or step off the path. Keep me aligned with Your will, always.

DAY 19

> I can do all things through Christ which strengtheneth me.
>
> PHILIPPIANS 4:13

DAY 19
Deeper understanding of my authority in Yeshua
Philippians 4:13

Lord, help me to realize the authority that I have in You.

When I was baptized in Your name like so many others in Your word, I took on Your authority. But I never fully recognized it. I never really understood it.

Teach me, Lord, the authority that I have in You, to battle the enemy, to have no fear, to worry for nothing, to walk confidently and boldly to lead the lost to You.

Teach me, Lord, the power of my words and the power of things spoken in Your name.

When I walk in Your authority, I will not fear. I will be anxious for nothing. I will break the enemy's back as I snatch souls from the greedy gates of hell.

For that is my purpose. It is the purpose of all who choose to follow You, to live for You.

You called us disciples. You told us the wondrous things that we will do in Your name.

And it is the reason that You give Your authority to all who go down in the water in Your name – who are obedient to Your word, to your commandments because we love You.

I thank You for this authority, Your authority. Make me a wise steward and teach me how to use it.

For I truly can do all things through You who strengthens me.

DAY 20

> As every man hath received the gift, even so minister the same one to another, as good stewards of the manifold grace of God.
> If any man speak, let him speak as the oracles of God; if any man minister, let him do it as of the ability which God giveth: that God in all things may be glorified through Jesus Christ, to whom be praise and dominion for ever and ever. Amen.
>
> 1 PETER 4:10-11

DAY 20
Understand my spiritual gifts
1 Peter 4:10-11

Lord, You said that everyone has received gifts from You. Your word says that we are to use these gifts to minister to each other and to reach the lost.

I want to be a good steward of the manifold of Your grace so help me to understand my own spiritual gifts.

Help me to know them and understand them. Help me to know how to use them for Your glory.

Put others in my path who will help me understand my gifts and use them effectively as You would have me use them.

I know that my gifts are to be used to serve You but I want to know what You want from me. Guide me in Your plan for my life. Help me to know and understand Your will and how I can walk in it.

I only want to serve You.

I only want to please You.

I don't want to squander what You have so freely given and I don't want to hide my light.

I want to be a light to the world so that people can see You through my life. I want my life to be a living testimony and that means knowing my gifts and using them according to Your will for my life.

I want to be obedient.

I want to glorify You.

DAY 21

> And the Lord make you to increase and abound in love one toward another, and toward all men, even as we do toward you: To the end he may stablish your hearts unblameable in holiness before God, even our Father, at the coming of our Lord Jesus Christ with all his saints.
>
> 1 THESSALONIANS 3:12

DAY 21
Put the love of God in my heart
1 Thessalonians 3:12

Lord, I ask You to put the love that You have for people, even my enemies, in my own heart. I want to feel the love that You have for them, for all souls. I want to know that unconditional love, the depth and breadth of loving someone so much that no matter what they do to me I can forgive them.

Love them so much I grieve for them when they are lost and rejoice with them when they find Your sweet salvation.

I want to have that love that compels me to go out and reach the lost, the unwanted, the forgotten.

Lord, I want to love the lepers!

Help me to love those who are hard to love, the forgotten, the ignored, the rejected, the abandoned.

Give me an understanding of them so that I can minister to them in the way they need. I want to show them Your face in my words and actions. I want them to see who You are and realize the immense love that You have for them – no strings attached.

I want to love them through the hurt, the anger, the depression, and help them find You in the midst of their storm.

I ask You let me see people through Your eyes and love them through Your heart.

For that unconditional, Christlike love is holiness.

And I want to be holy as You are holy.

DAY 22

> But the fruit of the Spirit is love, joy, peace, longsuffering, gentleness, goodness, faith, meekness, temperance: against such there is no law. GALATIANS 5:22-23

DAY 22
Purify me so that I may embody and display all the fruits of the spirit
Galatians 5:22-23

Lord, I ask You to cleanse me and purge me of anything within me that offends You.

Mold me, shape me, form me into what You want me to be. My life is Yours.

Kill off the parts of me that are not pleasing to You and fill me with You. Fill me with Your spirit so that I may have a new life, a new song, a new tongue, a new outlook.

And let Your Spirit work in me so that I may bear good fruit.

Lord, I want to bear the good fruit of love, joy, peace, longsuffering, gentleness, goodness, faith, meekness, and temperance. All of these are a reflection of Your own nature.

When I am bearing the fruit of Your spirit, I will be more like You.

For all of these things, all this fruit, are what You are and what I long to be.

Crucify this flesh! Cut off the things that do not please You, those things that keep me from bearing that good and holy fruit. I want to die to self so I can live fully with You. I want to present myself as acceptable to You.

I know that the way to do that is to reflect Your nature, to be more like You.

For the more I am like You, the less I am like me.

And the closer I get to being holy as You are holy.

Teach me to bear good fruit!

DAY 23

> For we wrestle not against flesh and blood, but against principalities, against powers, against the rulers of the darkness of this world, against spiritual wickedness in high places.
>
> EPHESIANS 6:12

DAY 23
Deeper understanding that everything is spiritual
Ephesians 6:12

Lord, increase my understanding of the reality of my walk with You.

I am created in Your image and Your word says that You are a spirit.

Since I am created in Your image, I am a spirit first and foremost. This means that the bulk of my battle is in the spirit.

And every battle begins and ends in the spirit.

This fleshly body is just a vehicle to get me through this world. My spirit is my true life and it abides in You.

Help me Lord, to keep my mind in the awareness that people are driven by the spiritual. If they have not submitted to Your spirit, the Holy Spirit, then they have submitted to something else and that is what I am dealing with.

They don't have to know it or be aware it is happening. They think those thoughts are theirs. Help me to remember the prison they are in because they are bound to a spirit that is not Yours.

Help me to remember this and help me maintain my love for the soul that is bound. Give me compassion for the prisoner and help me so that I can help them break free from their chains.

So instead of getting angry with the person, help me to remember that my battle is not with them, that they are prisoners.

I am battling the spirit that oppresses them – and it wants to keep them bound.

Teach me to set the captives free!

DAY 24

> Behold, I give unto you power to tread on serpents and scorpions, and over all the power of the enemy: and nothing shall by any means hurt you.
>
> LUKE 10:19

DAY 24
Realizing my power to defeat the enemy
Luke 10:19

Lord, I know that You said You gave me the power to tread on serpents and scorpions and over all the power of the enemy, but sometimes I just feel so helpless!

I need You to help me fully realize the power and authority that I have in You to defeat the enemy.

Help me to understand true warfare and make me Your soldier.

Give me discernment and understanding so that I can identify the enemy, know how to fight it, and emerge victorious.

And give me the knowledge and ability to share this with others so that I can teach them how to have victory over the enemy. I want to be able to help others escape those prisons and teach them how to break free, how to defeat the enemy, and how to have true spiritual warfare.

But it starts with understanding that You gave me Your power and Your authority to walk in every day so that I would be equipped to deal with whatever the enemy throws at me.

I know that it means being baptized in Your name and walking as You walked.

I know it means adhering to Your WHOLE word and living it as closely as I can. Only then will I be able to walk in that power and authority?

Open my understanding. Plow my heart. I want Your ways to become my ways so that I can walk confidently in Your power and authority in every area of my life.

DAY 25

> Submit yourselves therefore to God. Resist the devil, and he will flee from you.
>
> JAMES 4:7

DAY 25
Be more fully submitted to the Holy Spirit
James 4:7

Lord, I know You called me out of the world. I know that You want me to walk in Your ways – walk as You walked, but sometimes it is hard.

Sometimes I slip into my old carnal, worldly ways and don't even realize it until I am already there.

I face so much temptation every day. I want the devil to flee from me and Your word says that he will do this if I am submitted to You.

Deepen my understanding. I am committed to You but I need to be fully submitted to You, to Your Holy Spirit.

Your word says that it is Your spirit that will comfort me, guide me, and open my understanding of You. I want to walk as You walked and do all that I can to please You, but I can't do it alone.

I need Your spirit. I need to be filled with Your spirit. I need to understand, to know, what it means to be fully submitted to You.

I need Your spirit to guide me, help me, fill me so that the devil cannot even find a toehold within me. I want the devil to flee from me because the light inside of me is so much greater than what the world, his kingdom, could ever produce.

Help me separate from the world, Lord! Make the things of the world detestable to me because they are detestable to You.

Then help me get past myself so that I can rest in You, fully submitted to You.

DAY 26

> And be not conformed to this world: but be ye transformed by the renewing of your mind, that ye may prove what is that good, and acceptable, and perfect, will of God.
>
> ROMANS 12:2

DAY 26
I am separate from the world
Romans 12:2

I know that the world is not my home and I should be separate from it. I know that I am not to love the things of the world because that makes me an enemy to You.

Sometimes it is hard though because I do live *in* the world. But I must always remember that I am not *of* the world. And that is where I struggle sometimes.

Help me to separate myself from this evil world. Show me the areas that I need to work on, the parts of me that are still bound to a world that I no longer belong in.

Root out those things within me that are detestable to You. Reveal them to me and cut them off – kill them – so that I may be pleasing and acceptable to You.

I command carnality to go in the name of Yeshua!

I take control over my own flesh and bring it into submission to my will so that I may be submitted to Your will.

Help me to remember that there is nothing good that is of this world and anything that may bring me enjoyment or entertainment is only temporal and can be a doorway that leads me away from You.

For Your things are eternal and good and holy. Your things feed me, edify me, and allow me to fulfill my purpose in You.

Those are the things that I seek. Help me be wholly separate and apart from the world so that I can be holy as You are holy.

DAY 27

> My brethren, count it all joy when ye fall into divers temptations;
> Knowing this, that the trying of your faith worketh patience. But let patience have her perfect work, that ye may be perfect and entire, wanting nothing.
>
> JAMES 1:2-4

DAY 27
Help me weather the storms better
James 1:2-4

I know that storms are inevitable. They are going to happen. You said in Your word that there would be trials and difficulties.

You also said that as long as I am faithful and obedient to You that You would never forsake me.

And when the storms come it's human nature to get anxious or scared or flustered. But help me to remember that I can always run to You, even wake You from slumber and You will speak to the storm, "Peace be still."

I want that peace in ME so that when the storm is raging around me I can rest and know that You have me in the palm of Your hand.

Help me to look for the lessons in the storm so that I can weather them better and walk away stronger, wiser, and more rooted in You.

Help me learn to look to You first when difficulties come. Help me remember to always seek Your will in my life even if it doesn't look like what I expect or want.

I want to remember that You know best and You know what is best for me. Help me to stop getting in my own way. I want to give my life over to You so that I can have a deeper relationship with You.

Help me to walk in Your ways, the way You walked. Show me the obedience You seek in me and call me to more.

I don't want my will, but Your will to be done. I just need to stop trying to hold onto that control. I need to trust You to guide me in Your time and in Your ways.

Help me weather the storms with grace and peace that can only come from You.

DAY 28

> Wherefore, my beloved, as ye have always obeyed, not as in my presence only, but now much more in my absence, work out your own salvation with fear and trembling.
>
> PHILIPPIANS 2:12

DAY 28
Working out my own salvation
Philippians 2:12

I want to keep my mind set on You so that I do it Your way and not my own. I don't want my own perceptions and ideas to seep in, polluting Your word and hindering my salvation and growth in You.

Give me eyes to see and ears to hear so I can learn Your ways, Your thoughts and grow to have Your nature.

Plow my heart, make me teachable so that I can receive Your word, even when it is contrary to my flesh.

Especially when it is contrary to my flesh.

Don't let me get in my own way. Show me what I need to lay down and what I need to pick up in order to walk in Your ways.

Kill off those things within me that are not pleasing to You. Reveal them to me and kill them so that they no longer separate me from You – so that they no longer prevent me from growing in You.

I want to be pleasing to You, always.

I want to be obedient to You. Help me keep a right attitude so that I can walk in that obedience. Give me the courage and the strength to do this because I know that is hard to come out of the world.

Give me the perseverance and steadfastness to walk in Your ways because I know that they are so different from what the world believes.

I just want to please You.

I understand that I am the only one who is responsible for working out my salvation. Help me to do that, even if it means leaving all that I know and am accustomed to behind.

It is all worth it to walk with You forever.

DAY 29

> Speak unto all the congregation of the children of Israel, and say unto them, Ye shall be holy: for I the Lord your God am holy.
>
> LEVITICUS 19:2

DAY 29
Be holy as He is holy
Leviticus 19:2

I want to be holy as You are holy. I want to be holy as You have commanded me to be.

I know that means putting away the things of the world. Give me the courage and strength to do whatever it takes to walk with You in holiness.

I know that faith without works is dead. I want to show the world my faith by my works so that others can see You within me.

Guide me through Your word so that I can be holy as You are holy. Bring Your word to life and let it burn as a fire within me.

I know that I cannot be holy if I don't take action. I know that in order to be holy I must keep Your statutes and walk in Your ways.

Help me to understand those statutes and set my feet in Your footsteps. I want to walk as You walked. I want to walk in holiness.

Search me, see me, root out those things that do not please You. Purify me and give me a heart of flesh.

And as I lay down each thing of the world, help me to see that my identity is rooted in You and not in those things – not in my position in the world.

Let me see myself through Your eyes, the ugly and the beautiful, so that I may begin to nurture what is beautiful and starve what is ugly.

If I am going to come out of the world as You commanded, I am going to have to starve, to kill those ugly things that are the remnants that keep me bound to a world that should not want me.

I want to be transformed by You, by Your word, by Your love. For that is how I will be holy as You are holy.

DAY 30

> I am the vine, ye are the branches: He that abideth in me, and I in him, the same bringeth forth much fruit: for without me ye can do nothing.
>
> JOHN 15:5

DAY 30
Help me to abide in Yeshua
John 15:5

I want to abide in You.

I MUST abide in You for that is the only way I will be saved.

And by abiding in You I must keep Your statutes and walk as You walked.

Illuminate Your walk so that I may follow it. Open my eyes to see that it isn't what I want or how I feel or what I like or what makes me comfortable.

It's about what YOU have called me to do, to be.

You are the vine and I do not want to be separated from that. But in order to remain with You and grow in You, I must be obedient to You.

You said to keep Your commandments only if I love You. Help me to see those commandments, to understand them, to hunger for them and the life that they bring.

Show me the blessings of keeping Your commandments.

You said if I abide in You then I will walk as You walked. Help me to see beyond myself, my own limited, biased view, and find You and Your ways.

Help me to reach beyond any false teaching I may have encountered or inaccurate interpretations I may have formed on my own as I allowed my flesh to override the guidance of Your spirit.

Move me out of the way so that I can abide in You – so that I can be holy as You are holy and stay rooted in You.

Help me grow and bear much good fruit.

DAY 31

> Even so every good tree bringeth forth good fruit; but a corrupt tree bringeth forth evil fruit.
> A good tree cannot bring forth evil fruit, neither can a corrupt tree bring forth good fruit.
> Every tree that bringeth not forth good fruit is hewn down, and cast into the fire.
> Wherefore by their fruits ye shall know them.
>
> MATTHEW 7:17-20

DAY 31
Help me bear good fruit
Matthew 7:17-20

Help me to walk in such a way that others will know me by the fruit that I bear.

I want to bear good fruit. I don't want to be cast into the fire. Help me to discern between good fruit and corrupt fruit.

I know that the view of good fruit has been skewed by false teachers and those who fail to study, so open my eyes and show me true good fruit.

As I study Your word, ingest it, write it on my heart. Let it work in me, changing me, so that my fruit is good and I can be a good witness.

Give me a testimony! Change the fruit that I bear so that it reflects Your holiness within me.

I don't want the world's interpretation of love, joy, peace, longsuffering, gentleness, goodness, faith, meekness, and temperance – I want the true definition that is Yours.

I want to love as You love.

I want the joy and peace that can only come from You.

I want Your patience, gentleness, and goodness toward others so I can lead them to You.

Strengthen my faith so that I know, I KNOW, that as long as I am obedient and faithful to You, that You will NEVER leave me or forsake me. I want the faith that gives me the courage to break away from the world and loose myself of that bondage.

Help me to have meekness, to know who and what I am in relation to You.

And give me self-control to walk in Your ways and have the discipline to stay on this walk and always bear fruit that comes from Your holiness.

For that is how they will see You when they look at me.

ABOUT THE AUTHOR

Stephanie A. Mayberry is an author and freelance writer. She and her husband are pastors of a home assembly, Torah Observant Apostolics, in Baton Rouge, Louisiana.

She writes primarily for adult and young adult audiences in addition to teaching Bible studies as well as preaches and teaches to various groups. She also creates children's Bible lessons and activities.

Stephanie is involved in several ministries, including spiritual warfare and deliverance, healing from trauma, and ministering to adults and families on the autism spectrum (through her blog, The Christian Aspie, and several books she has written about being a believer with Asperger's Syndrome).

She also uses her personal experiences with domestic violence to minister to people who have been through abuse and help them find healing through Yeshua.

TorahObservantApostolic.org and ALifeOfHoliness.com.

www.StephanieMayberry.com

CONNECT WITH STEPHANIE A. MAYBERRY

Amazon.com/author/stephaniemayberry

Smashwords.com/profile/view/StephanieMayberry

Email: stephanie@thechristianaspie.com

Twitter: http://twitter.com/fotojunkie

Facebook: http://www.facebook.com/stephanie.a.mayberry

TorahObservantApostolic.org/

ALifeOfHoliness.com/

Like Stephanie's Facebook Author Page

Facebook.com/authorstephaniemayberry

Made in the USA
Columbia, SC
14 June 2024